102 ½ USES AN EXTRATERRESTRIAL

102½ USES FOR AN EXTRATERRESTRIAL

by
PAUL MAX RUBENSTEIN
CHRIS KRAJCI
ROBERT D'AMATO
FRANK CORONADO

Chicago Review Press   213 West Institute Place   Chicago

Copyright © 1982 by Paul Max Rubenstein, Chris Krajci, Robert D'Amato, Frank Coronado

All rights reserved
Printed in the United States of America
First edition
Published by Chicago Review Press, Chicago, Illinois
ISBN 0-914091-23-9

To Morris W. Rubenstein, Mel Brisk,
Mary Lou D'Amato, Marie Yanca, Frank Sr.
and Linda Coronado, and the Rubenstein family,
Michelle, Ari, Debbie, and Buffy and Arthing.

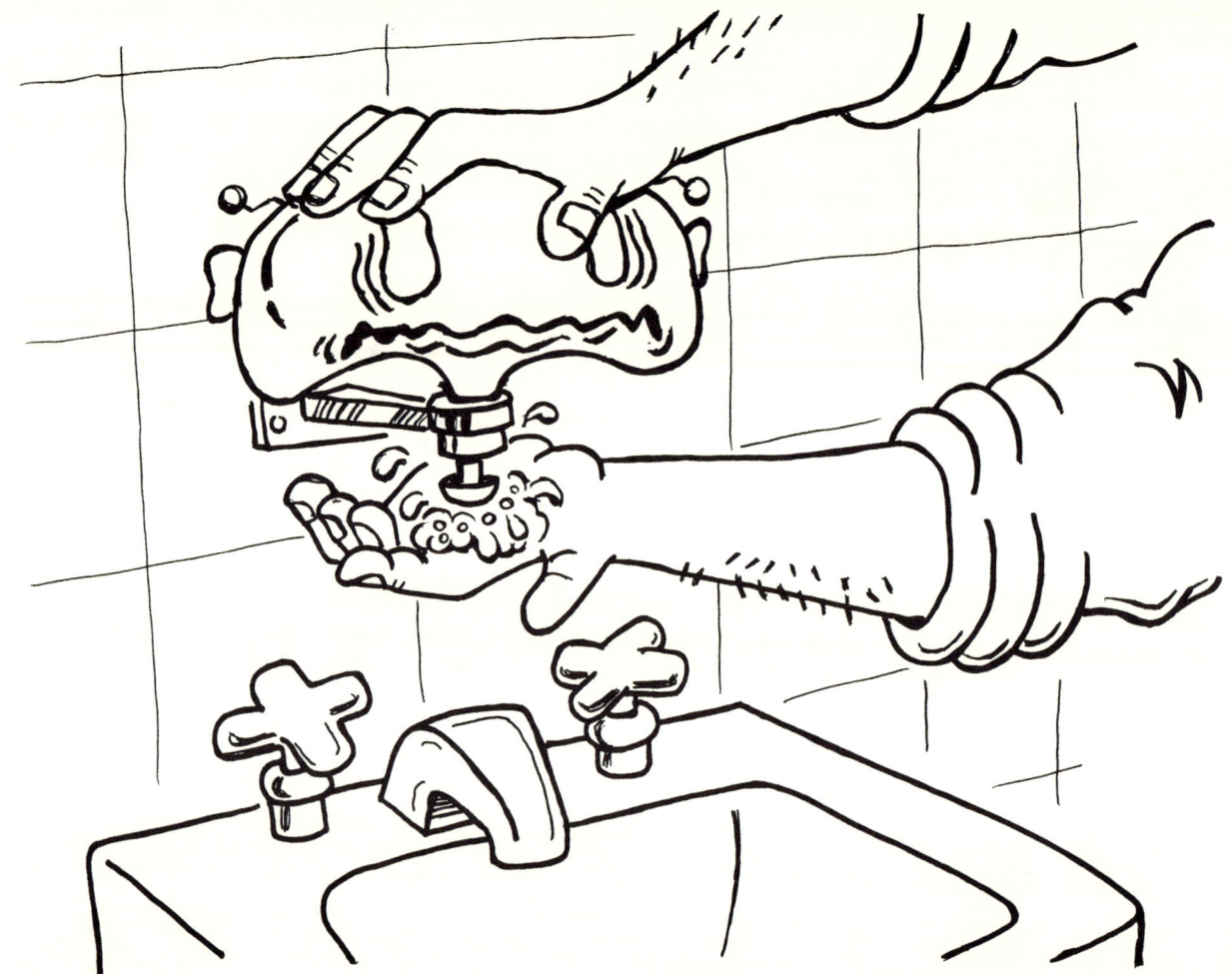

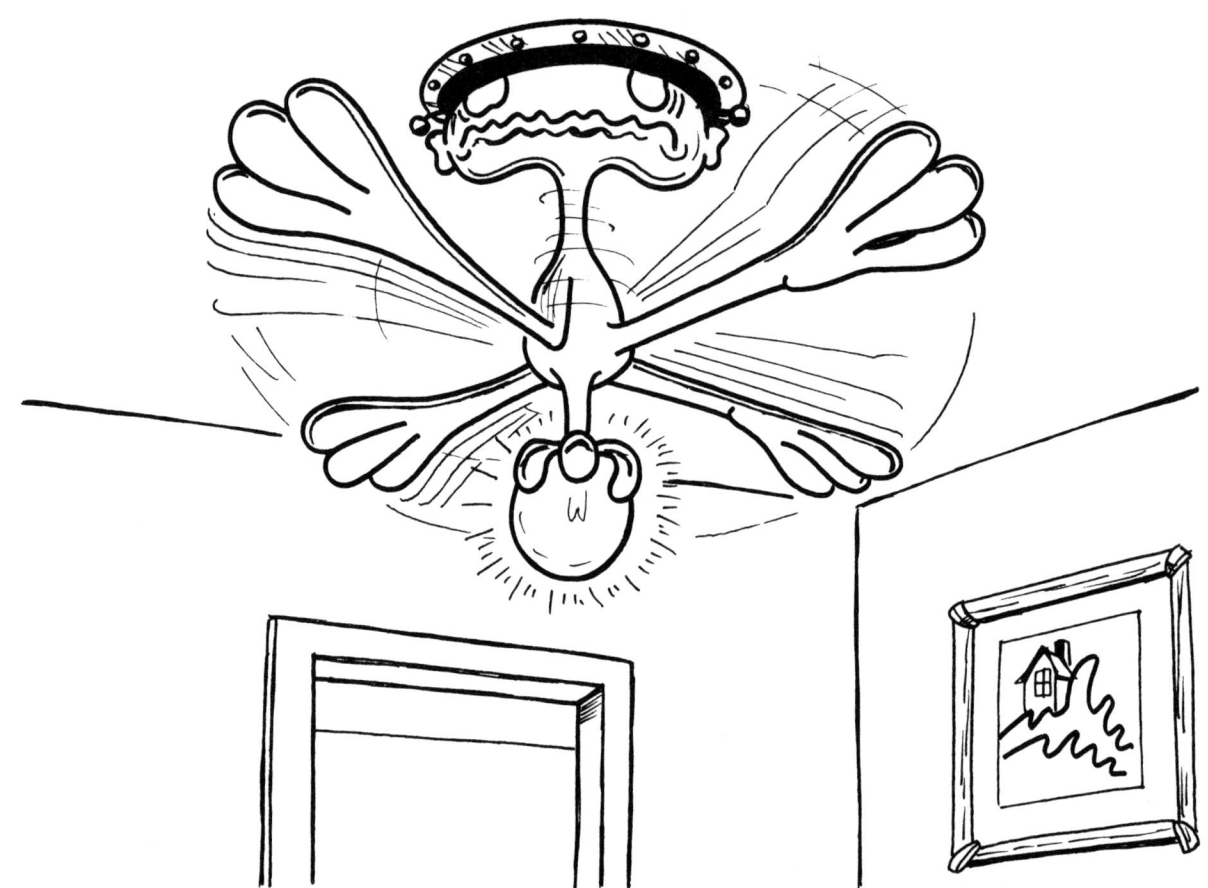

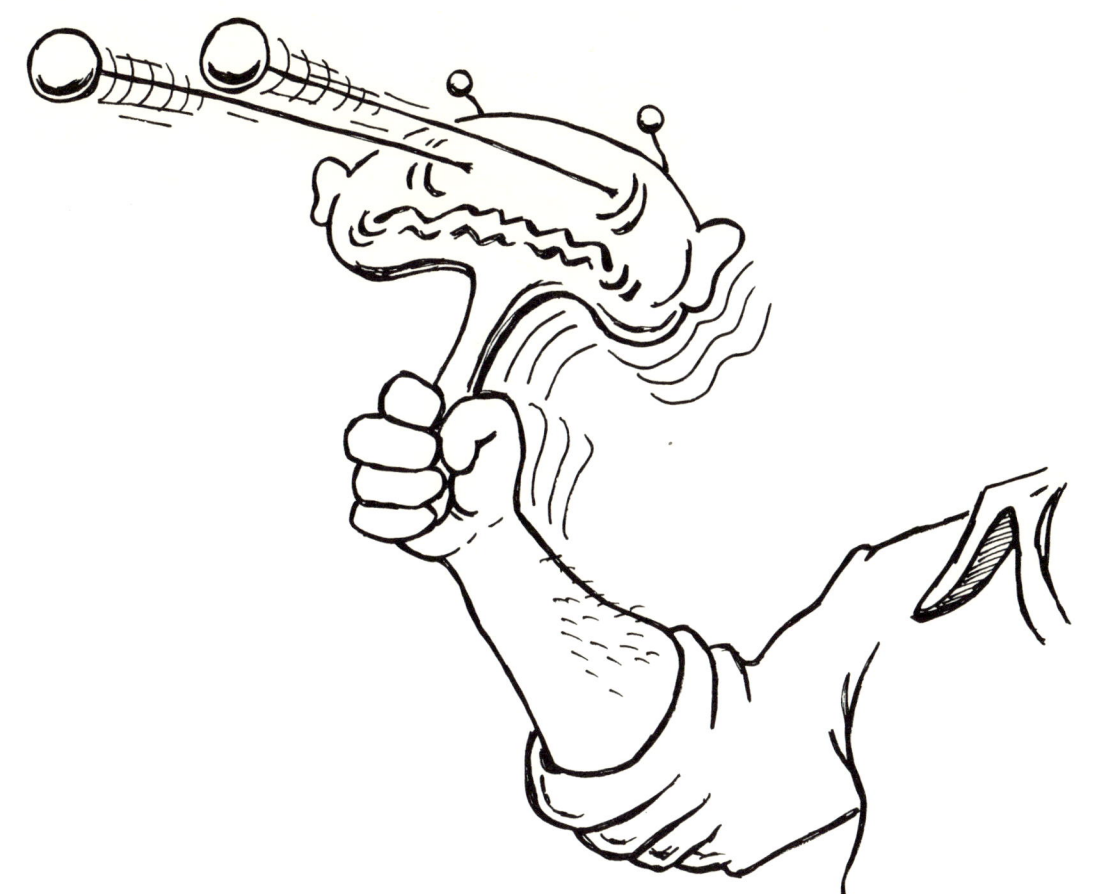

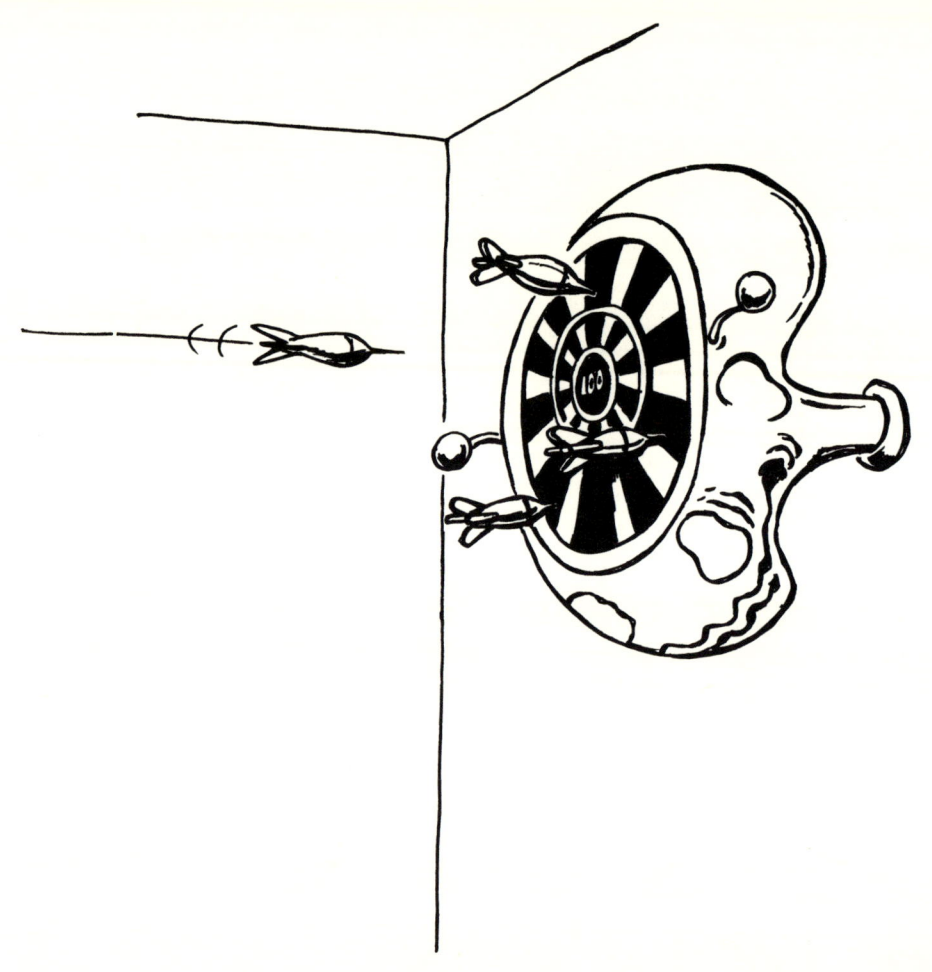

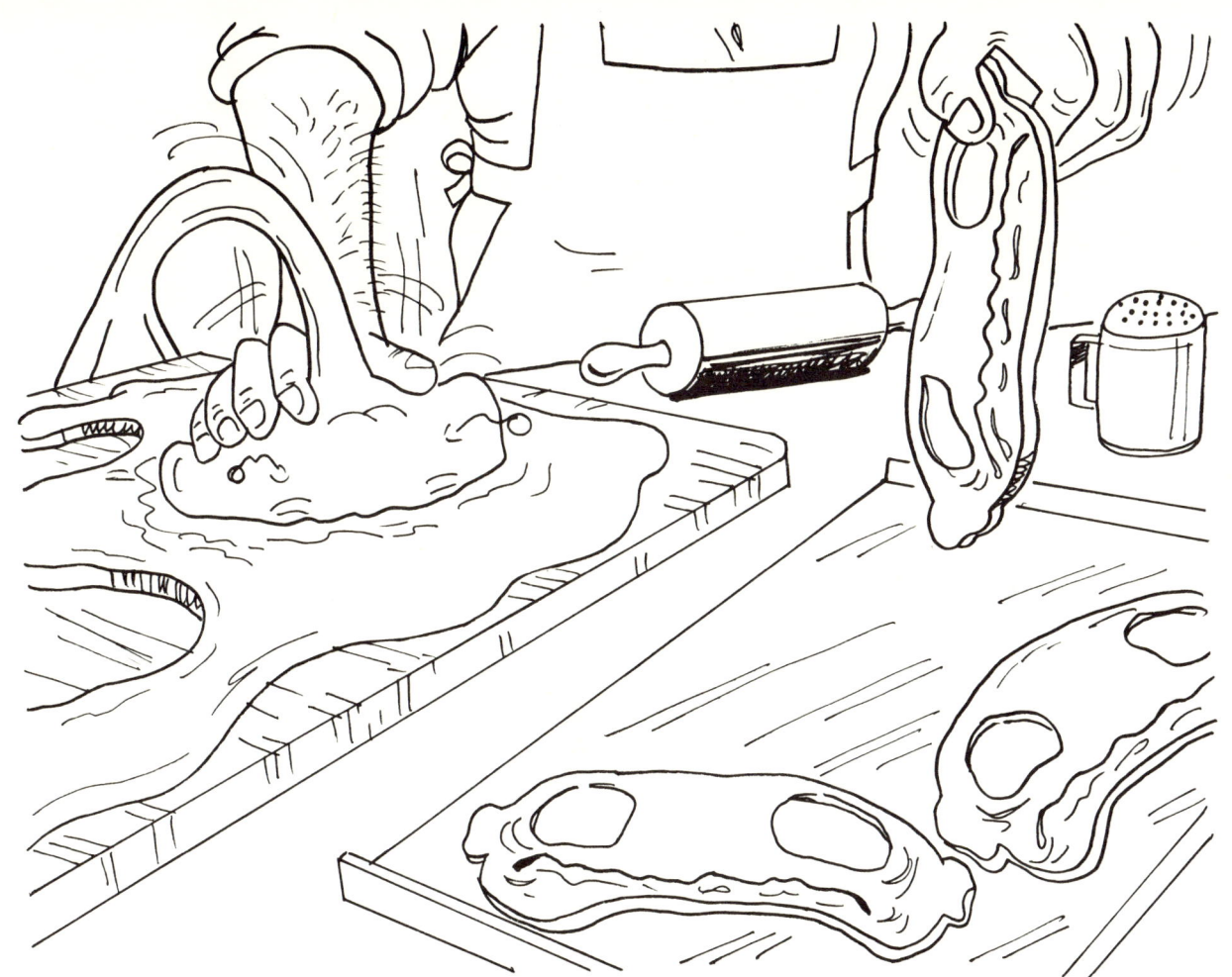

19

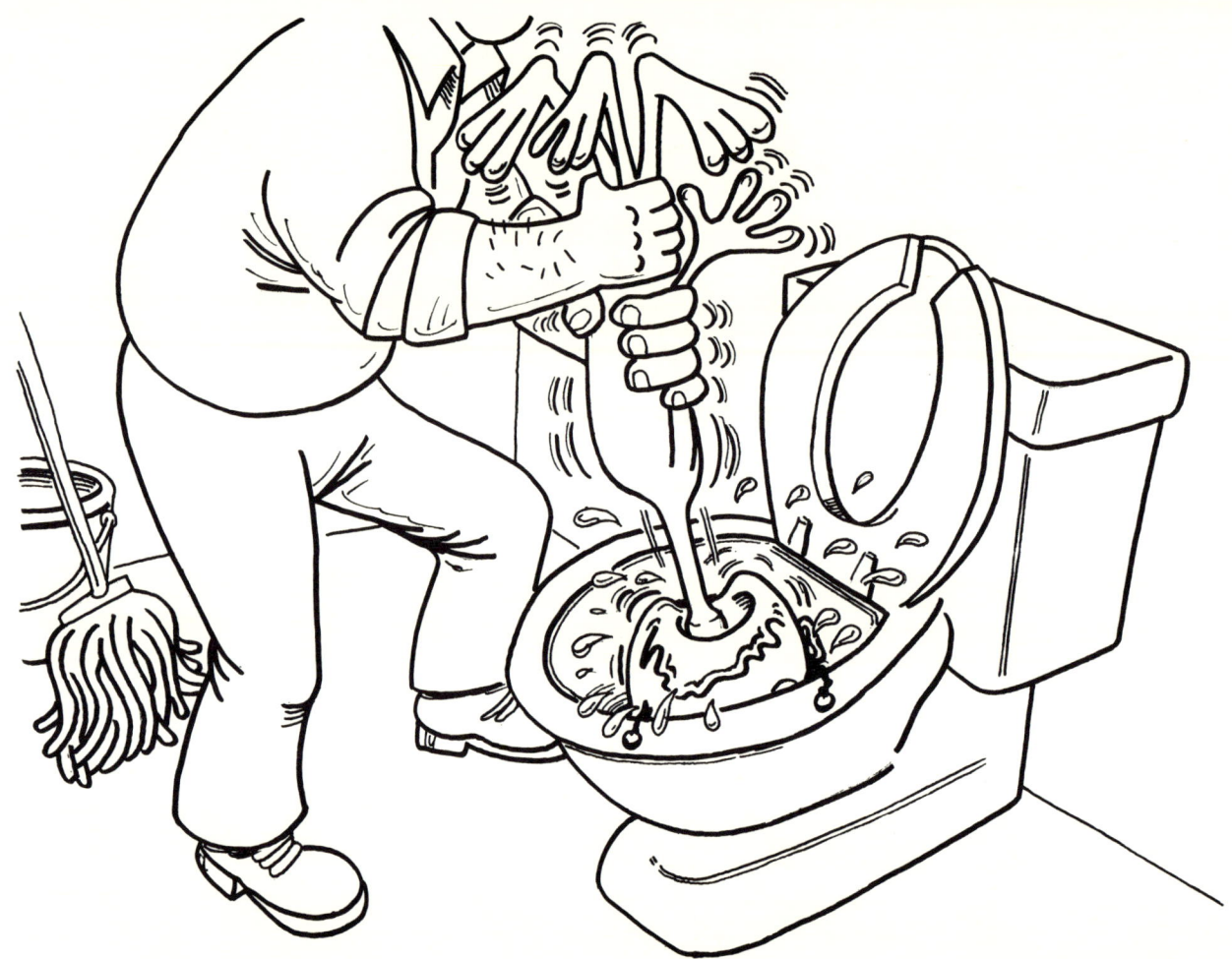

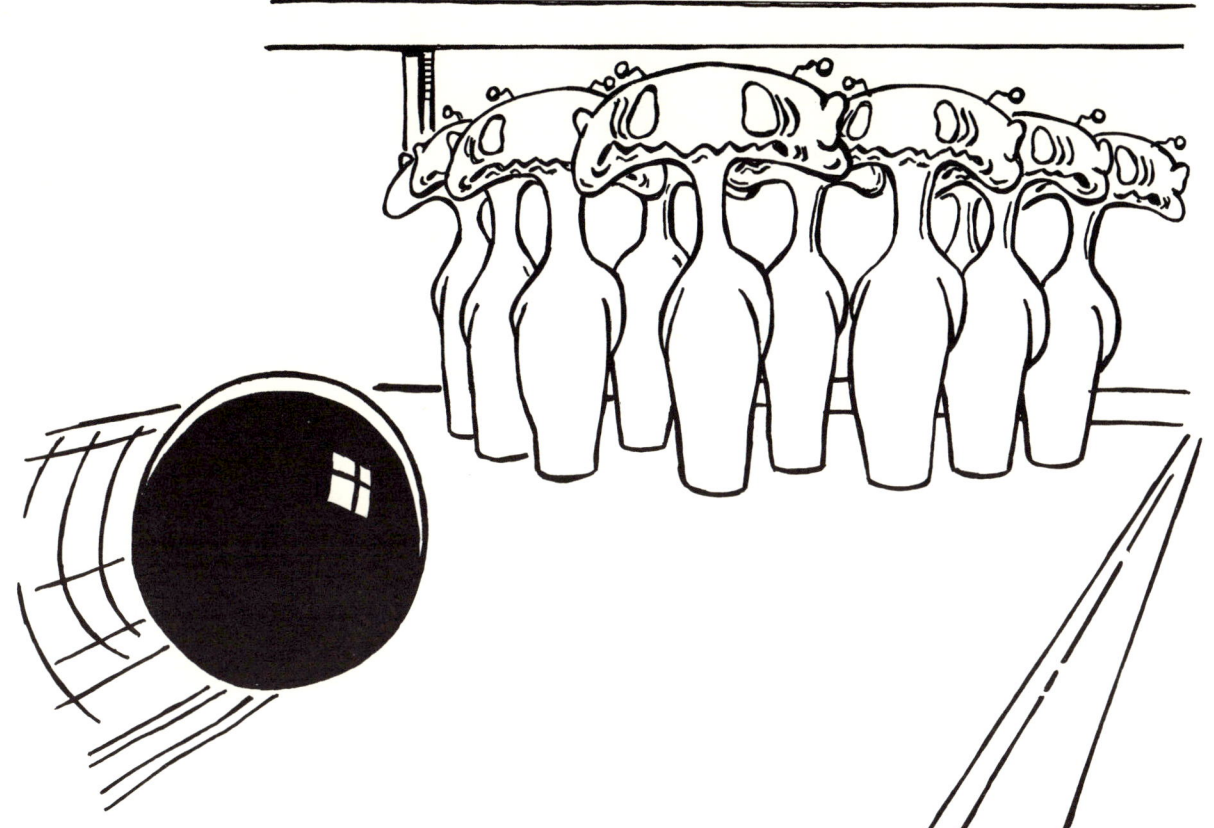

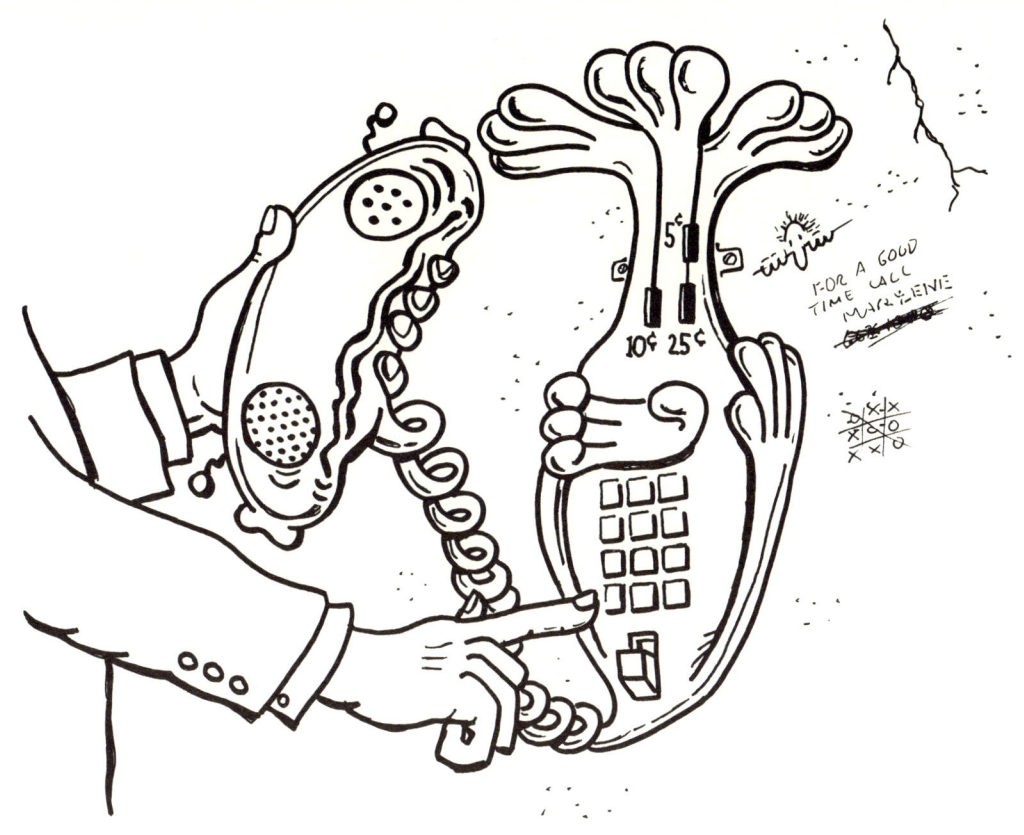

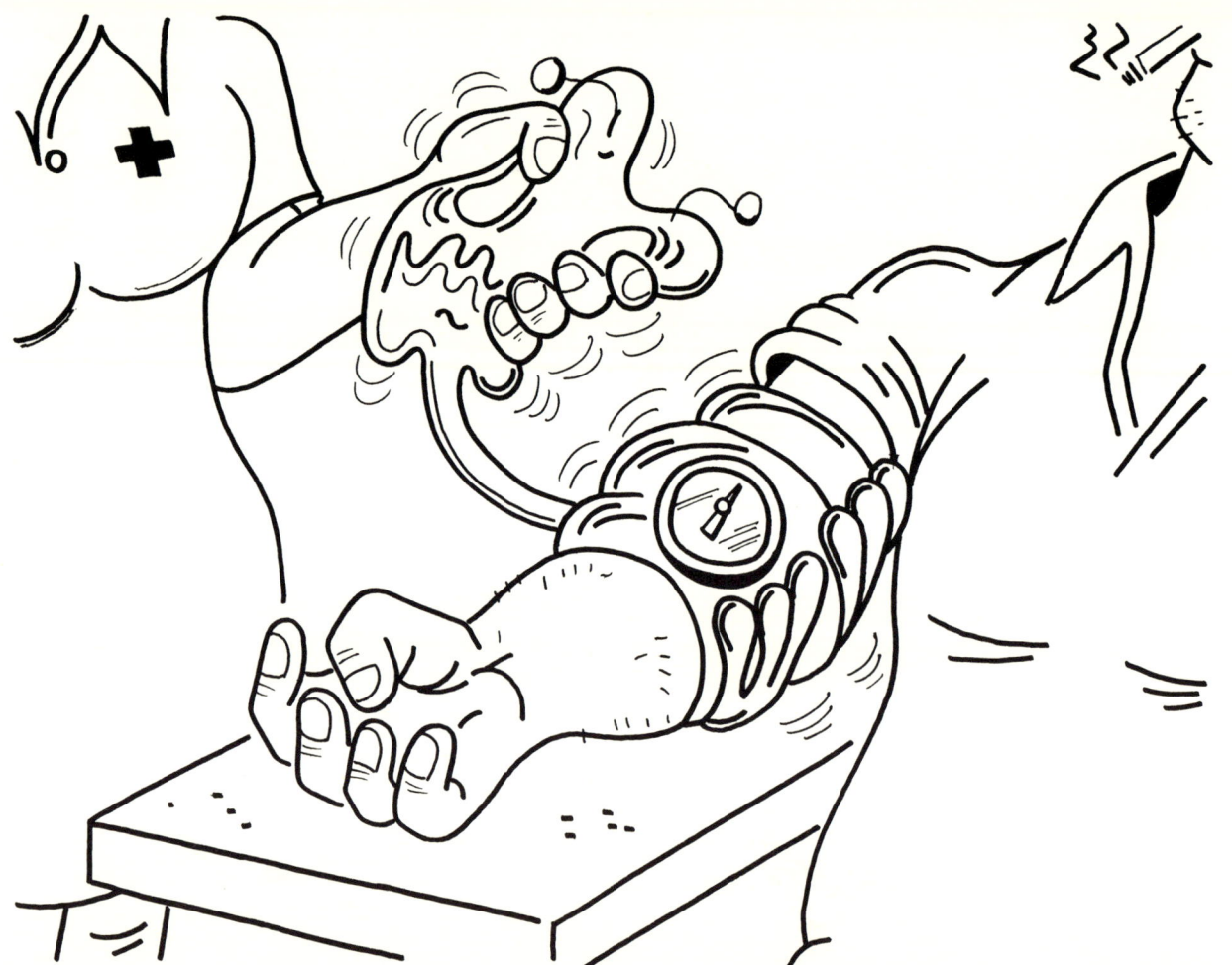

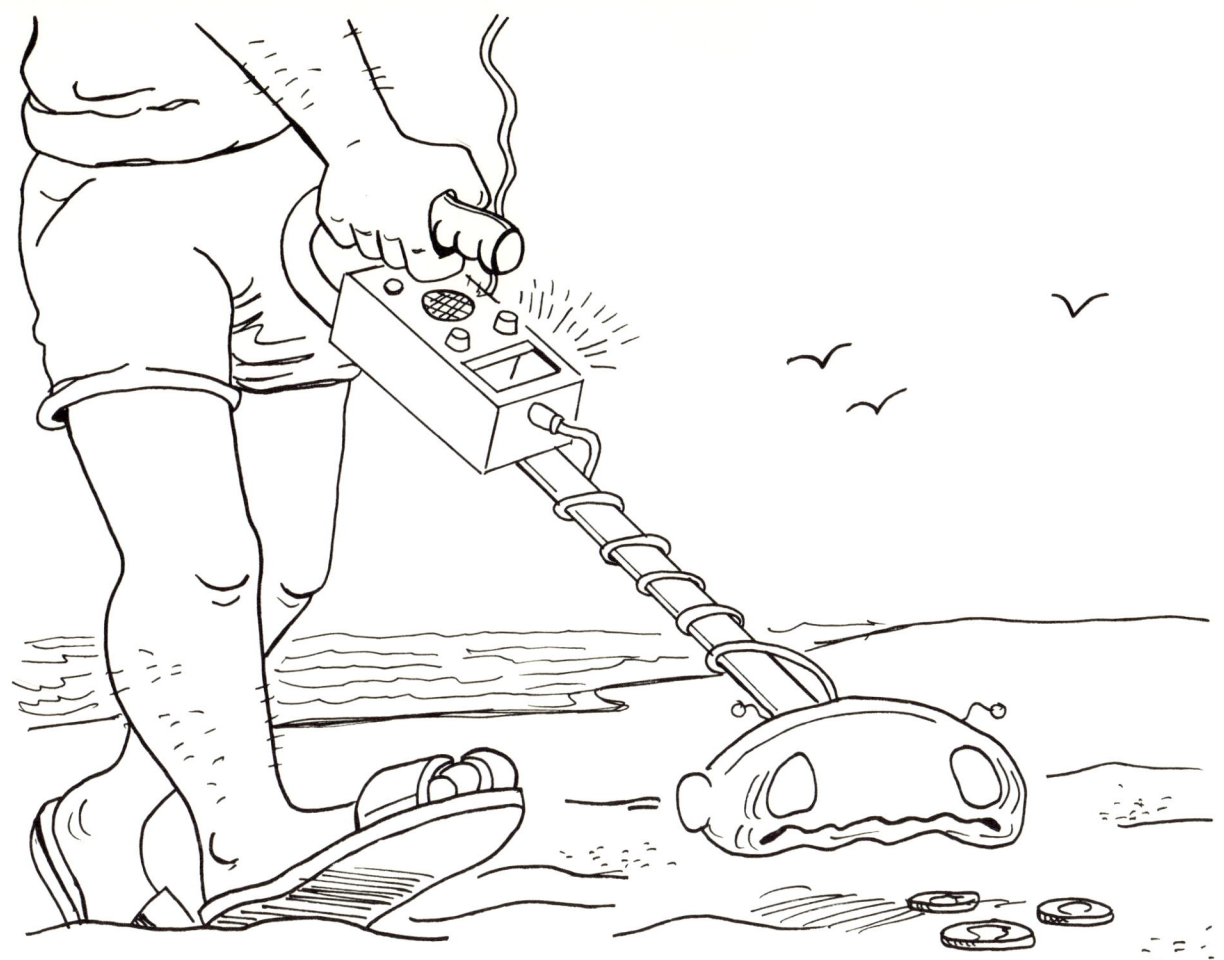

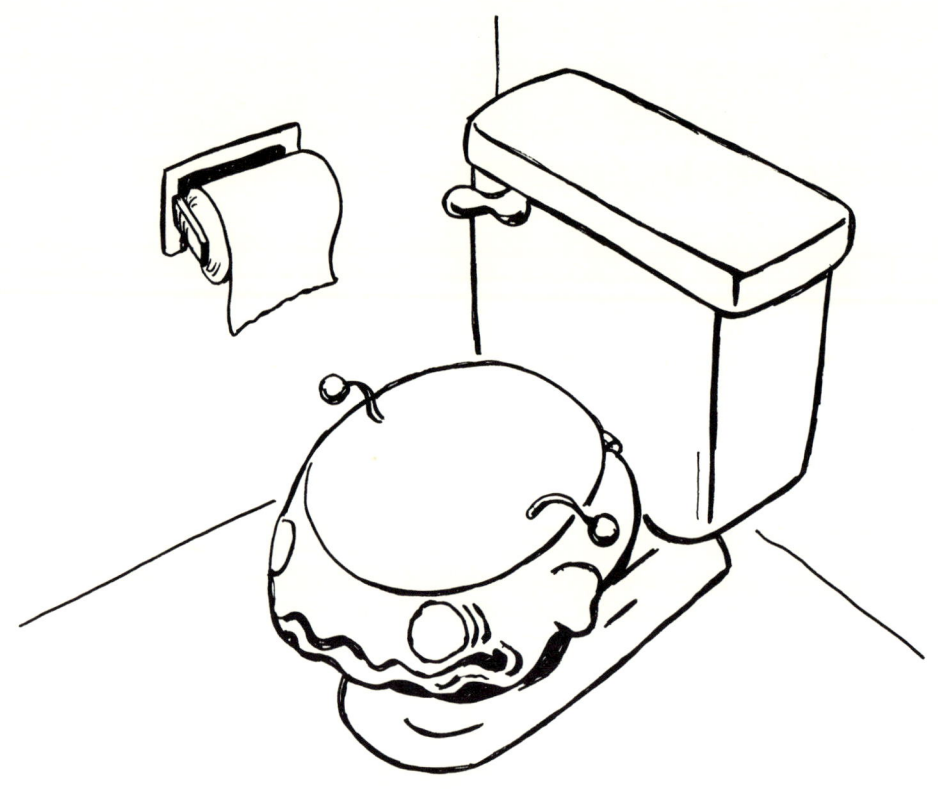

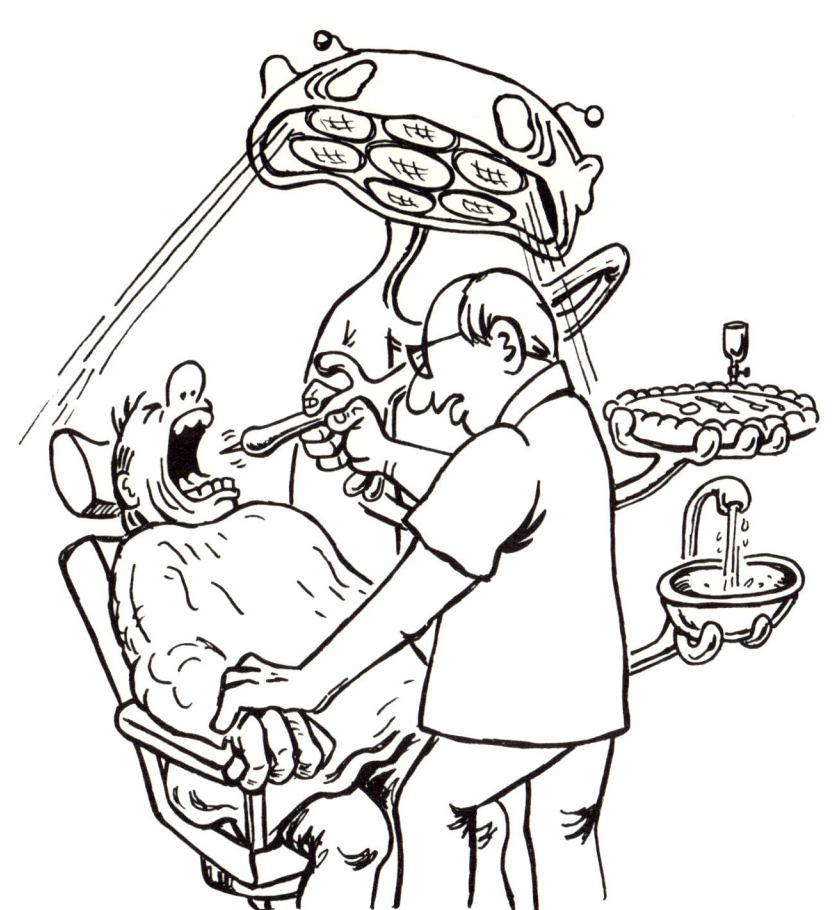

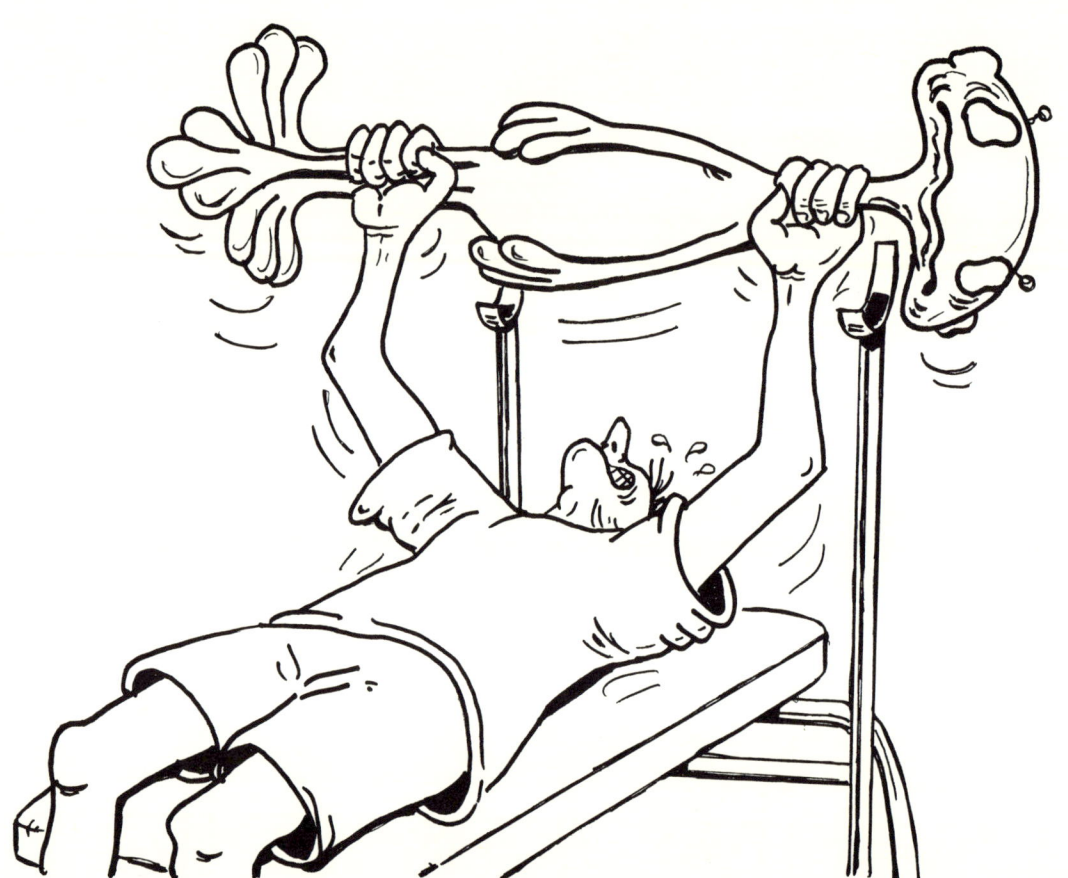

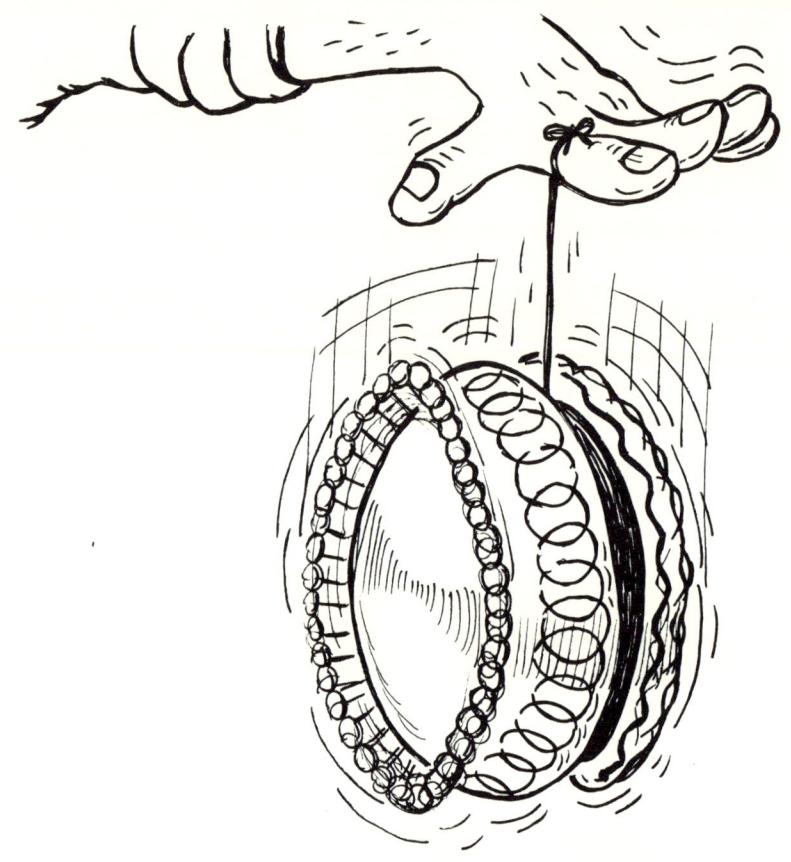

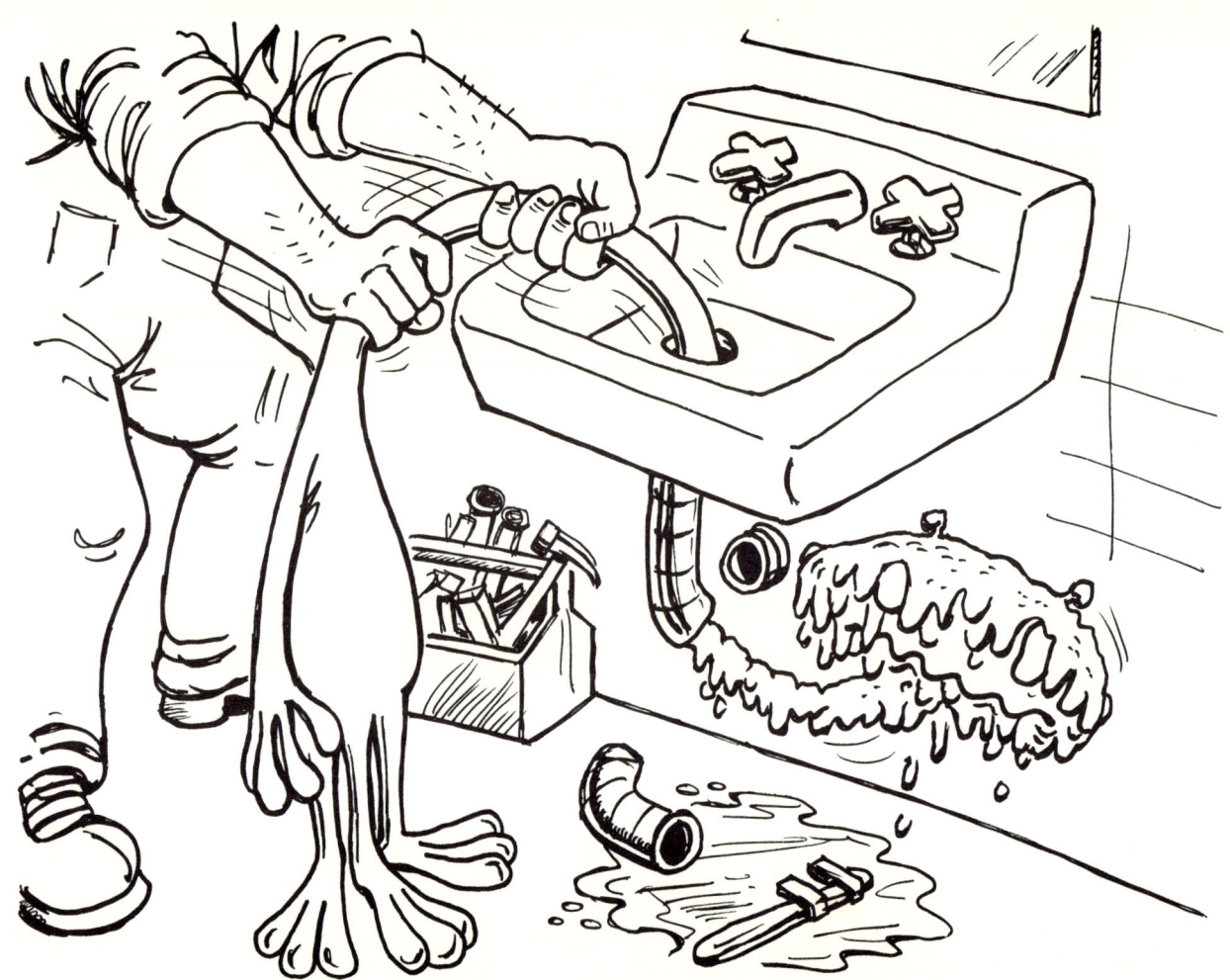

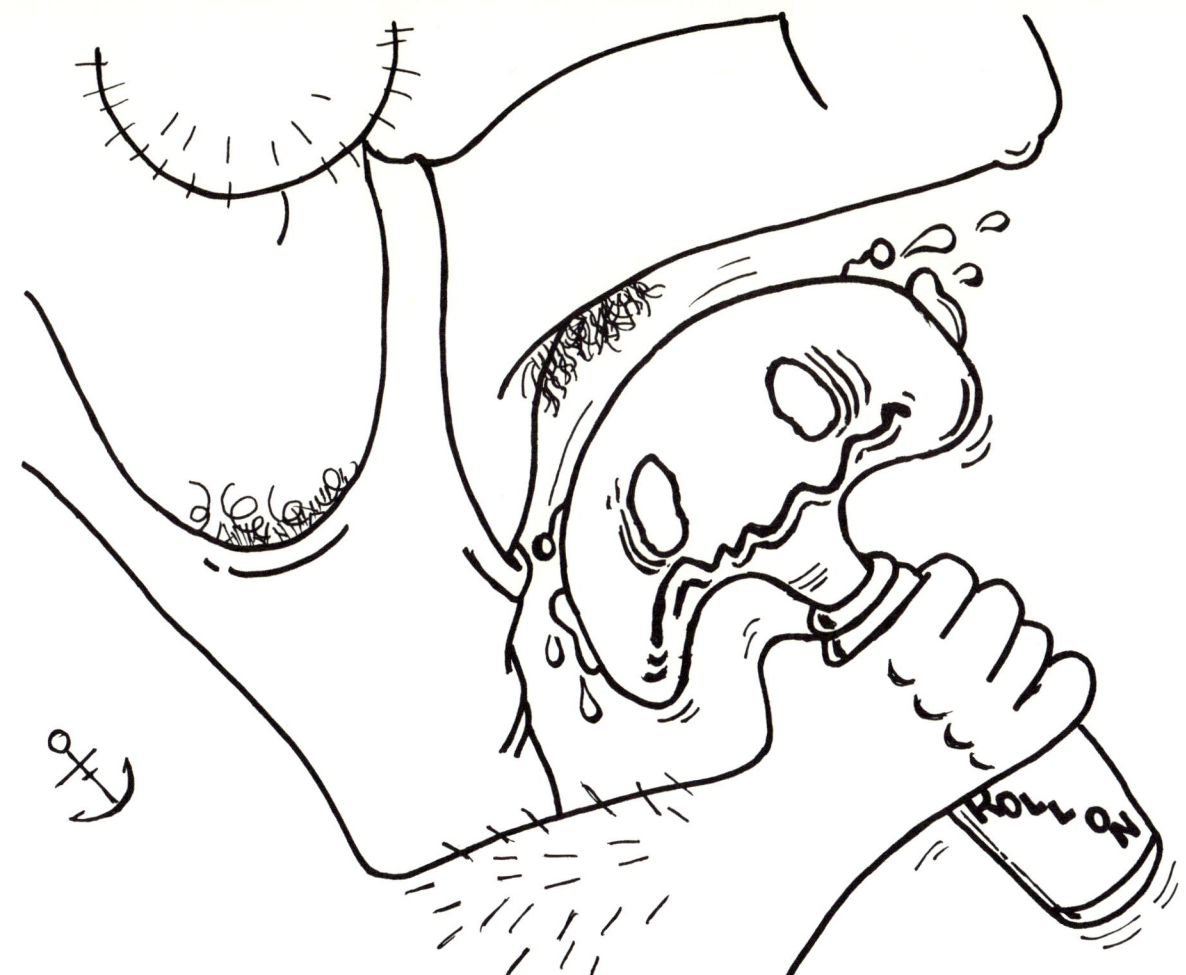

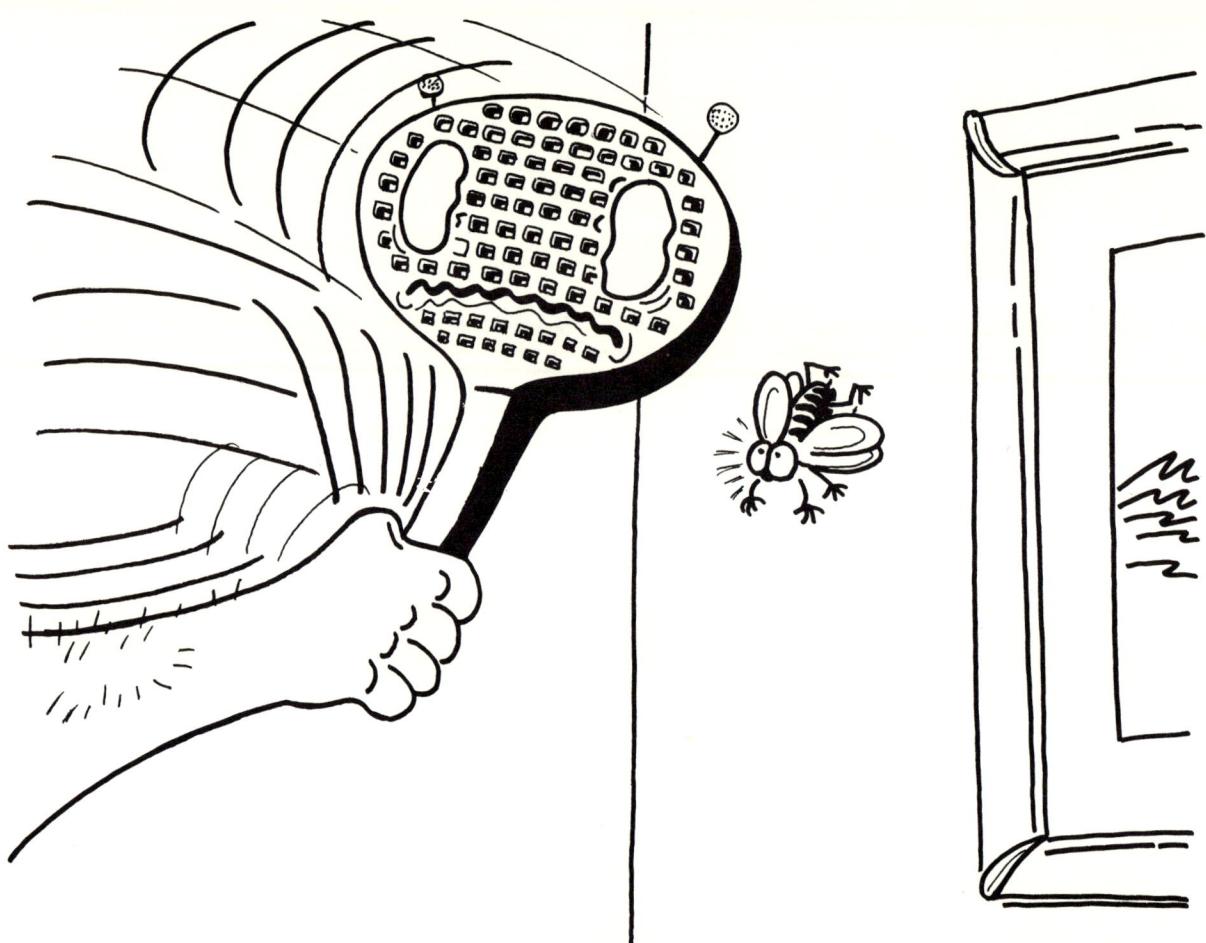

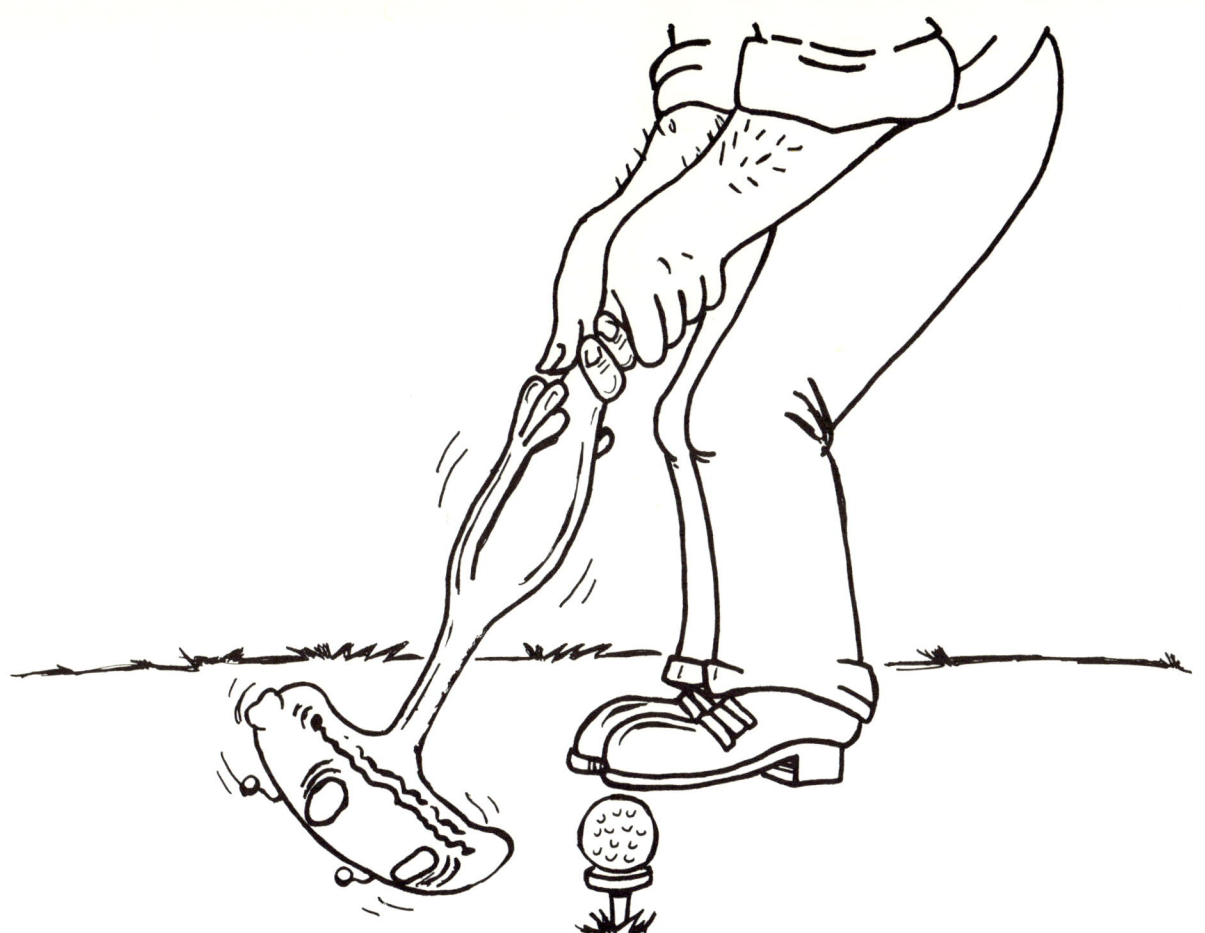

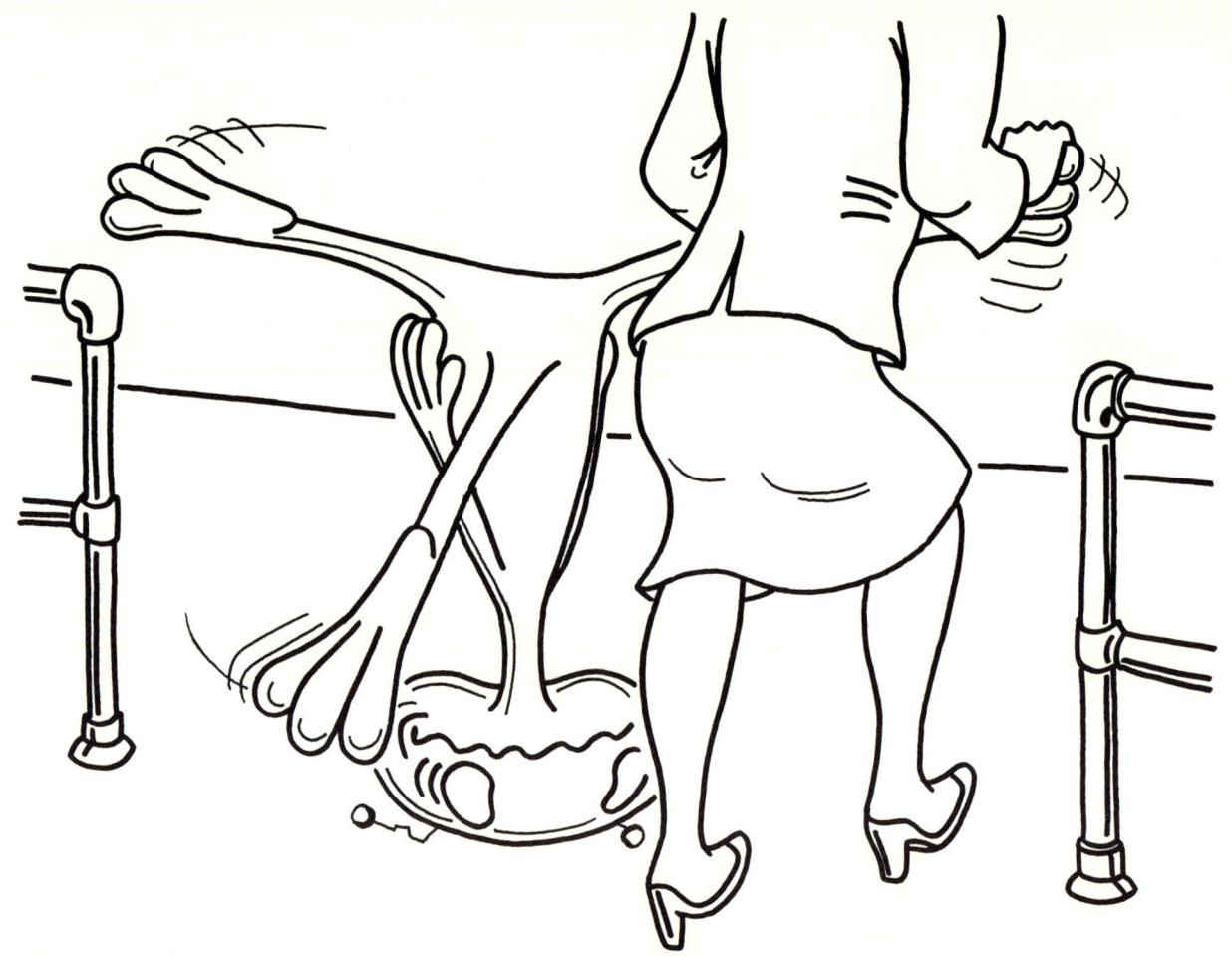

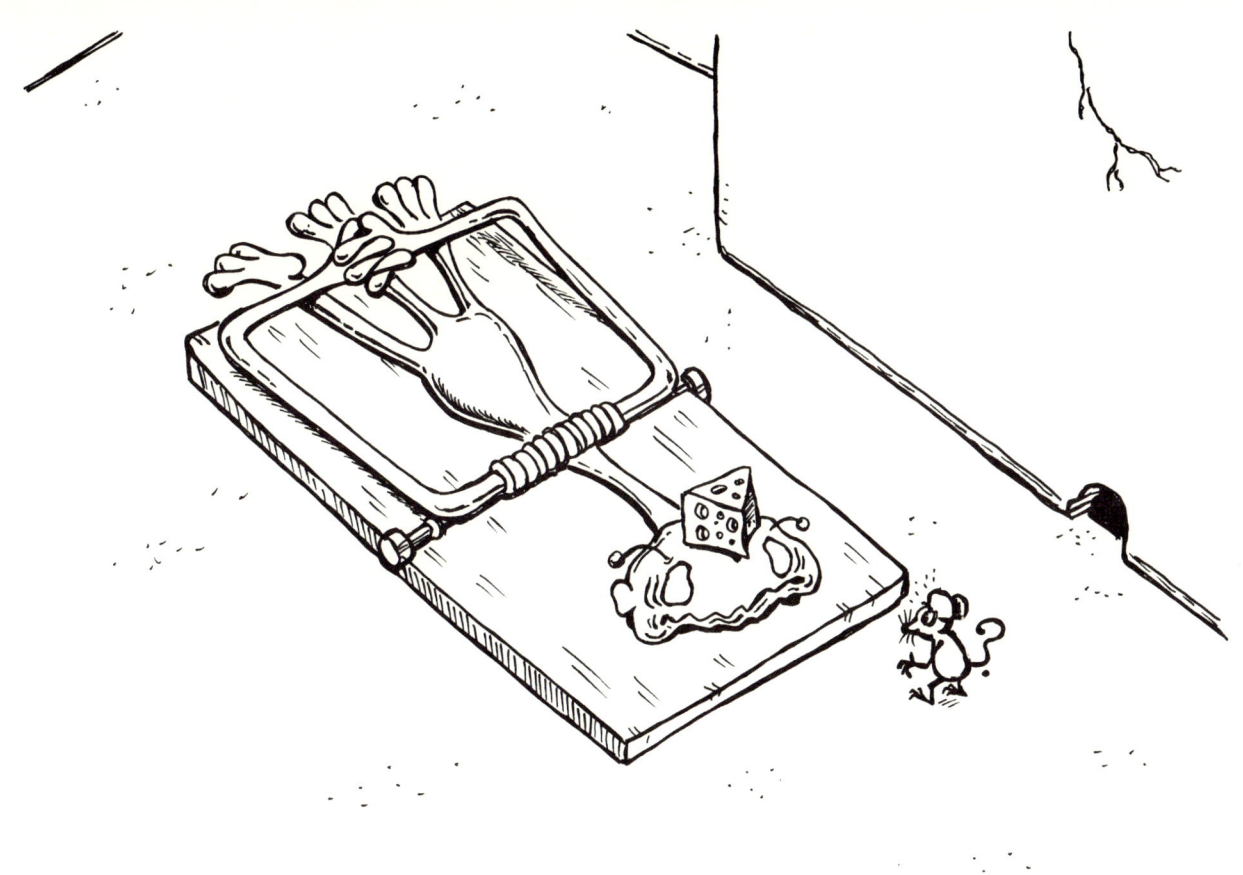

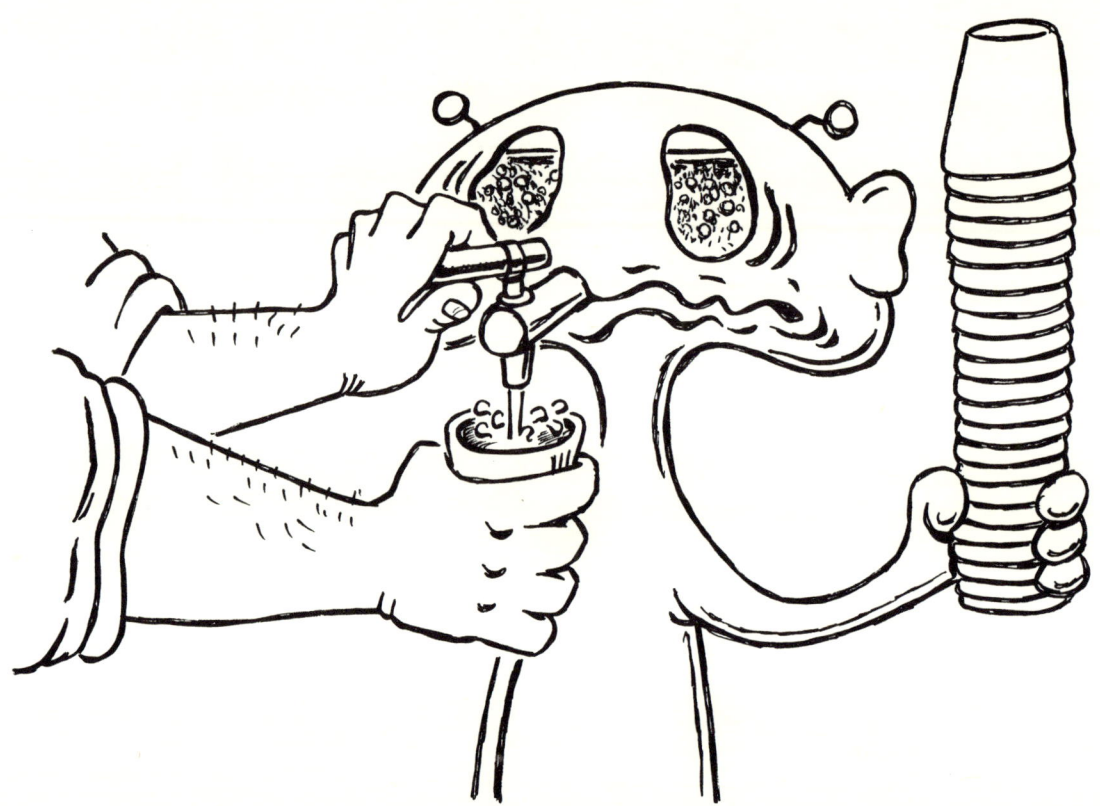

84

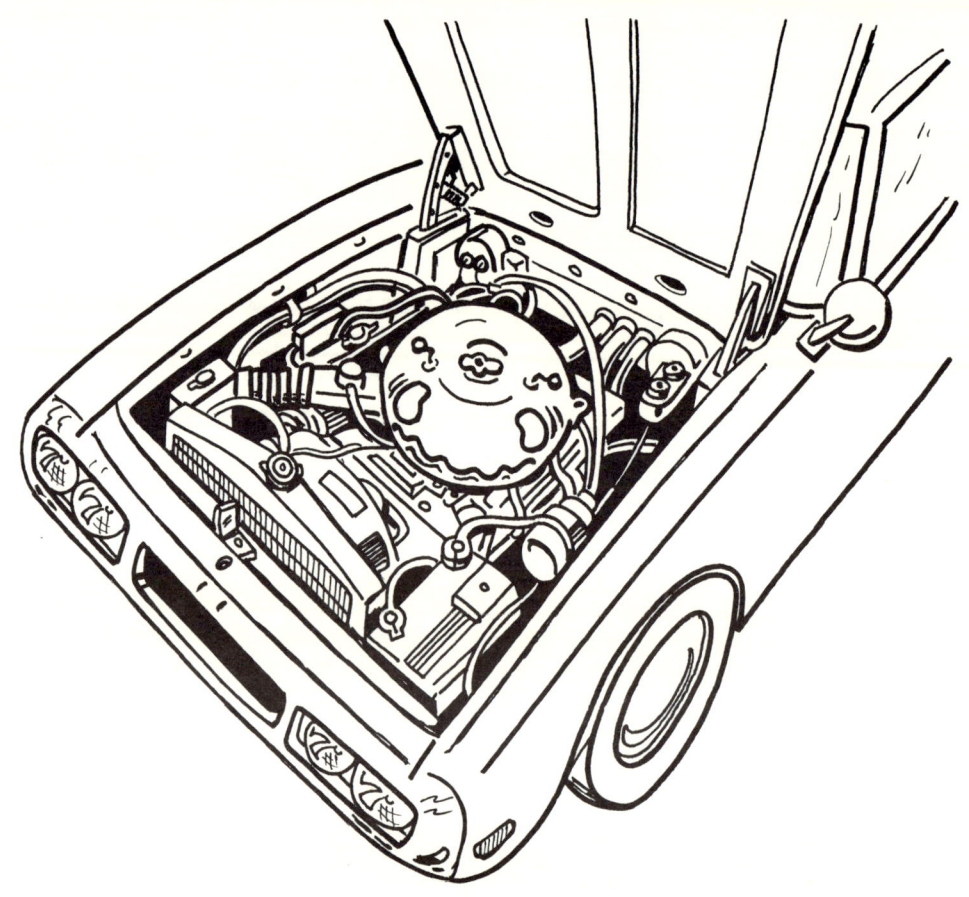

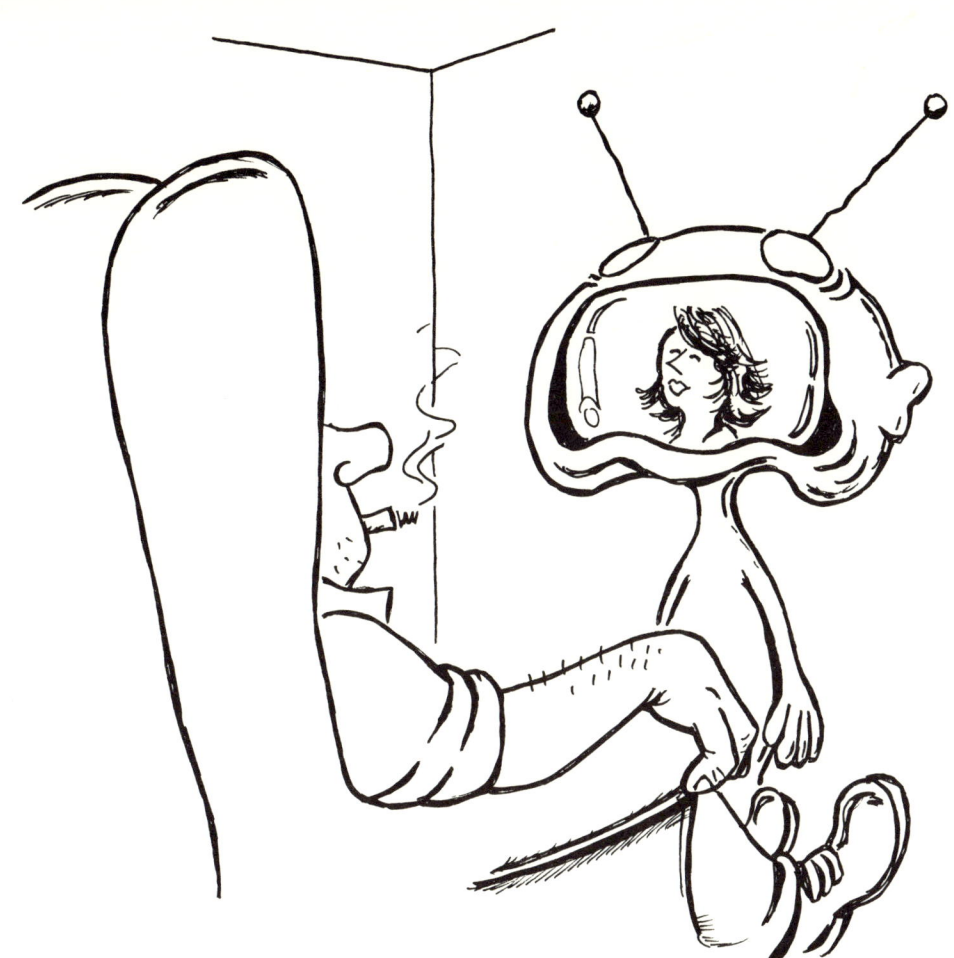

LIST OF ILLUSTRATIONS

1. Lawn sprinkler
2. Vacuum cleaner
3. Gas pump
4. Soap dispenser
5. Cork screw
6. Ceiling fan
7. Paddle ball
8. Ice cream scoop
9. Mona Lisa
10. Flag pole
11. Parking meter
12. Dart board
13. Stars from television series
14. Lawn jockey
15. Cookie cutter
16. Rock guitarist
17. Statue of Liberty
18. Jack o'lantern
19. Gearshift knob
20. Plunger
21. Horseshoes
22. Buoy
23. 10⅓
24. Drinking fountain
25. Peep show
26. Reading lamp
27. Car jack
28. Hot air balloon
29. Rockettes
30. Outboard motor
31. Rubik's cube
32. Wrecking ball
33. Bowling pins
34. Muffler
35. Guacamole dip
36. Camera
37. Bar stool
38. Extraterrarium
39. Taffy-coated alien
40. Candelabra
41. Railroad spike
42. Coat rack
43. Pay phone
44. Blood pressure
45. Doggie chew
46. Hang glider
47. Metal detector
48. Toilet
49. The thinker
50. Toll gate
51. Dentist's console
52. Barbells
53. President
54. Yo-yo
55. Ghetto blaster
56. Plumber's snake
57. Railroad crossing signal
58. Metronome
59. Olympic torch
60. Beach umbrella
61. Illegal alien
62. Cat scratching post
63. Accordion
64. Baby's rattle
65. Ice bag
66. Football
67. Hair dryer
68. Hamburger bun
69. Deodorant
70. Hand grenade
71. Bird cage
72. Fly swatter
73. Golf driver
74. Door knob
75. Drum set
76. Turnstile

77. Mousetrap
78. Christmas tree
79. Blow dryer
80. Water cooler
81. Extraterrestrial's roots
82. Pot-bellied stove
83. TV talk show host
84. Gothic column
85. Water tower
86. Barbecue
87. Crutch
88. Engine
89. Trumpet
90. Potter's wheel
91. Slot machine
92. Punching bag
93. Aqualung
94. Pin cushion
95. TV set
96. Inner tube
97. Flying disk
98. Ashtray
99. Turntable
100. Razor
101. Shotgun
102. Mt. Rushmore

102½. TV stand

ABOUT THE AUTHORS

Frank Coronado is a cartoonist, illustrator, writer, and terrestrial. His last illustrations were for Grime and Punishment.

Robert D'Amato is an artist, writer, comedy performer, whose works are still mostly unpublished on seven continents.

Chris Krajci is a twenty-three-year-old graphic artist, writer, and supermarket clerk who would like to be a twenty-four-year-old graphic artist, writer, and starship navigator.

Paul Max Rubenstein is the author of Writing for the Media, and a screenwriter for Universal Studios. He directs television commercials and teaches screenwriting at Columbia College in Chicago.